daily afflictions
daily afflictions
daily afflictions
daily afflictions
daily afflictions
daily afflictions
daily afflictions
daily afflictions
daily afflictions
daily afflictions
daily afflictions
daily afflictions
daily afflictions
daily afflictions
daily afflictions
daily afflictions
daily afflictions
daily afflictions
daily afflictions
daily afflictions
daily afflictions
daily afflictions
daily afflictions
daily afflictions
daily afflictions
daily afflictions
daily afflictions
daily afflictions
daily afflictions
daily afflictions
daily afflictions

Also by Andrew Boyd

LIFE'S LITTLE DECONSTRUCTION BOOK:

SELF-HELP FOR THE POST-HIP

THE ACTIVIST COOKBOOK

daily afflictions
daily afflictions
daily afflictions
daily afflictions
daily afflictions
daily afflictions
daily afflictions
daily afflictions
daily afflictions
daily afflictions
daily afflictions
daily afflictions
daily afflictions
daily afflictions
daily afflictions
daily afflictions
daily afflictions
daily afflictions
daily afflictions
daily afflictions
daily afflictions
daily afflictions
daily afflictions
daily afflictions
daily afflictions
daily afflictions
daily afflictions
daily afflictions
daily afflictions
daily afflictions
daily afflictions
daily afflictions
daily afflictions

THE AGONY OF
BEING CONNECTED
TO EVERYTHING
IN THE UNIVERSE

Andrew Boyd

W. W. Norton & Company

New York • London

Excerpt from "Dear Stranger Extant in Memory by Blue Juniata," from *The Book of Nightmares*. Copyright © 1971 by Galway Kinnell. Reprinted by permission of Houghton Mifflin Company. All rights reserved.

Excerpt from "Women and Honor: Some Notes on Lying," from *Arts of the Possible: Essays and Conversations* by Adrienne Rich. Copyright © 2001 by Adrienne Rich. Used by permission of the author and W. W. Norton & Company, Inc.

Submitted excerpts from pages 15, 175 from *Selected Poems of Rainer Maria Rilke*, edited and translated by Robert Bly. Copyright © 1981 by Robert Bly. Reprinted by permission of HarperCollins Publishers, Inc.

For information about permission to reproduce selections from this book, write to Permissions, W. W. Norton & Company, Inc., 500 Fifth Avenue, New York, NY 10110.

The text of this book is composed in Gill Sans Light
with the display set in Kabel Light
Composition by Molly Heron
Manufacturing by The Courier Companies, Inc.
Book design by Blue Shoe Studio
Production manager: Leelo Märjamaa-Reintal

Library of Congress Cataloging-in-Publication Data
Boyd, Andrew, 1962–
   Daily afflictions : the agony of being connected to everything in the universe / Andrew Boyd.
      p. cm.
   Includes bibliographical references.
   ISBN 0-393-32281-5 (pbk.)
   1. Affirmations—Humor. I. Title.

PN6231.A42 B69 2001
818'.5402—dc21

2001030940

W. W. Norton & Company, Inc.
500 Fifth Avenue, New York, N.Y. 10110
www.wwnorton.com

W. W. Norton & Company Ltd.
Castle House, 75/76 Wells Street, London W1T 3QT

1 2 3 4 5 6 7 8 9 0

To my brother void

We need the books that affect us like a disaster, that grieve us deeply, like the death of someone we loved more than ourselves, like being banished into forests far from everyone, like a suicide. A book must be the axe for the frozen sea inside us.

—FRANZ KAFKA

If you are going to tell people the truth, you had better make them laugh or they will kill you.

—OSCAR WILDE

contents
contents
contents
contents
contents
contents
contents
contents
contents
contents
contents
contents
contents
contents
contents
contents
contents
contents
contents
contents
contents
contents
contents
contents
contents
contents
contents
contents
contents
contents
contents
contents
contents
contents
contents

contents
contents
contents
contents
contents
contents
contents
contents
contents
contents
contents
contents
contents
contents
contents
contents
contents
contents
contents
contents
contents
contents
contents
contents
contents
contents
contents
contents
contents
contents
contents
contents
contents
contents
contents
contents
contents

The Book of Daily Afflictions is not unlike a book of psalms. Though dark, ironic, and irreverent, these afflictions are sacred poems that elevate and educate the spirit. Anyone acquainted with the many other books of daily meditations available today should find the format used here familiar. Each entry has a heading, a quote, a short message, and a closing meditation that you can repeat throughout the day. Likewise, this book's intentions are in perfect harmony with the best self-help traditions. It offers readers inspiration, practical advice, and food for thought as they navigate the jungle of existential terror and paradox that begins anew each day.

There are many ways to use this book. The easiest is simply to pick it up and open it at random, skipping around from affliction to affliction. Or you might scan through the table of contents and read only those afflictions whose titles look interesting to you. If you turn to the book in time of need, use the handy section headings—if you're having trouble in your family, for example, you can read all the afflictions in the section titled "Family." Alternatively, you might read the book straight through once then leave it by your bedside or toilet, going back to your favorite entries again and again. Several readers I know pull it off their bookshelf when they're particularly depressed and need a dose of cathartic despair. If you're more social, you may prefer to get together with friends and read the afflictions to each other.

Some readers have been so taken with The Book of Daily Afflictions that they have begun to create their own spiritual circles, centered around the book's message and teachings. In living rooms and rented halls across America, like-minded folks have been coming together in self-organized gatherings under various names, among them the Church of Skeptical Mysticism, the Temple of Ironic Faith, the Companions of Compassionate Nihilism, and the Brotherhood of Brother Void. In these gatherings, The Book of Daily Afflictions has been used much like a book of psalms. Someone reads the whole affliction out loud, and everyone assembled repeats the closing line together. Participants have designed their own rituals and made their own rules. Some are more Apollonian, incorporating additional readings and spirited discussion. Others are more Dionysian, featuring testimony, chanting, and chaotic stomping. If you wish to join a circle in your area or begin your own, visit us at www.dailyafflictions.com, where we've established a clearinghouse for these efforts. Or just join our on-line virtual circle.

A final note to readers. This is not a book of daily *affirmations*. This is a book of daily *afflictions*. Although both kinds of books are affirming in their own way, they follow radically different approaches to affirmation.

Affirmations bathe you in light and manifest all that is positive. They promise that you can attract what you wish for by visualizing it. Afflictions make no such promises. They remind you that when you feel desperate and alone, you are. Afflictions mobilize the suppressed power of your dark side. If your inner child can help you cry again, just imagine what your inner critic, inner bigot, and inner psychopath can do to you.

You can't avoid suffering. The right affliction, however, can make your suffering more meaningful. It won't tell you the answer, but it can deepen an unresolvable question; it won't help you find yourself, but it might help you to realize that you are irretrievably lost. A strong affliction is profound yet painful. It reminds you that the truth will set you free, but first it will hurt like hell.

What afflicts one person, however, may not afflict another with sufficient severity. As you make your way through this difficult life, you must find the afflictions that are right for you. For only in darkness, light; only in paradox, truth; only in affliction, affirmation.

A canonical text is clear, concise, diamond hard. Its final appearance belies the process of its creation. Scattered around it lie the remnants cut away in shaping it. Forgotten are the stories, myths, and history that had to precede it; the hands of invisible authors; the lost years of a beguiling prophet. This Brother Void, what do you know of him? What can you tell from his picture? From hearing his voice on the radio? Or even from seeing him yourself—in a place of worship, an auditorium, or a living room—a dark sage illuminated in the blue glow of his laptop, his voice certain, his eyes long hallway eyes, looking into you? *I have seen things in the darkness, strange and rare.*

What of the years before he wore the cassock, before he came to the wisdom he now professes? What of his doubts, and, yes, his doubts about his doubts? I have known him across the years. I remember his salad days and after. I remember his torments at the hands of the divine. I remember the text—the day he began it, the many incarnations, the years of grinding it into shape. "Man," says Paul Tillich, "is asked to make of himself what he is supposed to become to fulfill his destiny." But how does any man, never mind a prophet, know what he is "supposed to become?" And how does he learn to become it? When once I asked Brother Void about these matters, he referred me to a favorite passage of his from the writings of Friedrich Nietzsche:

> In man, *creature* and *creator* are united: in man there is matter, fragment, excess, clay, mud, madness, chaos; but in man there is also creator, sculptor, the hardness of the hammer . . . *your* pity is for the "creature in man," for that which has to be formed, broken, forged, torn, burned, annealed, refined—that which has to *suffer* and *should* suffer.

It is among those fragments, that mud and madness, those hammer blows, that I believe we will uncover the story of Brother Void.

As with everyone, there was tragedy: he lost his only brother, he watched his father die. There was heartbreak, failure, confusion, and despair. There was also joy and victory. Through it all, he turned his twisted eye on his own suffering, condensing it into the harsh little bits of wisdom that make up much of The Book of Daily Afflictions. Yes, it was he who got "fucked by love" on page 40. It was he who got clobbered by a large planet at 29.6 years of age and wandered around for the next five years, repeating to himself, "I don't know what I'm doing but I'm doing it as hard as I possibly can."

Back when the book was a shapeless mass—before he had worked it over and over and over—his then-girlfriend called it his "complaint journal." If I were to retrieve the sheaf of jottings and early drafts from under one of the piles of books and papers in

Brother Void's monastic New York City apartment and read you the sprawling reflections from this journal—that now, as afflictions, are dense and taut, with just the right comic twist to hit home—you would find most of it prosaic and redundant. But there are some stories worth telling. He has faced down his own death. He has had visions—serious, industrial-strength visions. He did what Nietzsche tells us not to—he gazed too long into the Abyss—and Nietzsche was right, the Abyss gazed back into him.

The surprising humor of The Book of Daily Afflictions has sometimes distracted even the most astute and sober readers from the dogged truth-telling that lies behind it. But it would be a mistake to underestimate Brother Void. Whether he is "Embracing his inner corpse," or experiencing "The agony of being connected to everything in the Universe," I believe he is not making less or more of these things than they actually are.

When it comes to the subject of God—however named, or unnamed—Brother Void has earned the right to say a few words, and we owe him the honor of listening.

———————

It is fitting that his first vision occurred in the desert. It is fitting to the point of irony that the desert carried the name Death Valley. There he was, a young man barely 20, tromping around the desert like a fool. It was getting late, he was trying to make his way back to camp. The desert air had cooled considerably. He was hurrying against the closing twilight, scrambling down a gully—fast, and then slow, and then fast again—sliding on his ass down a crease of broken sandstone, loose rock spilling alongside him. A narrow twist and the ravine steepened. He turned around. With his back to the dimming sky, he worked his way down. He was moving faster than was wise. He noticed his error too late.

Fear flicked up through his legs. He pressed his weight into the rock, instinctively, hands and feet needling deeper into their holds. The rock wall dropped down and away. There was nothing beneath him but empty air. For the first time, his life was completely in his own hands.

He held on to the rock for long moments. His past collapsed behind him; his future lay truncated on the rocks below, its head cut off from Time. There was only death, wafting under him in the empty air. Nothing before this had been real. It was as if, for years, he had been held in a protected field, a set-up life, and now death had cut away the false foundations. He had never faced death before, but he could feel now that it had always been there—a fearsome abyss holding life in its empty fist, just as the empty air held him now.

He had to move. He was excruciatingly in command. He had to step deeper into his terror and further out over the void. There was no other way. To his left was a rounded outcropping of rock and on the other side of it a means of descent. *Make for over there.* He let go of his left handhold and slipped off one strap of the backpack, then switched hands, then slowly the other strap. He let the pack fall down to the rocks below. In some far-off place, in some unreal time, he hoped the flashlight had not broken.

Then slowly, he began to inch his way left cranny by cranny, hold by hold. He made slow, careful progress. He was halfway across. With the toe of his sneaker he felt out the loose-fitting rock in the next cleft. He kicked away at the broken bits of rock. Nudging his way in, he tested its strength. It was okay. He transferred his weight over to it. It held. He trusted it, committed to it. All his weight, now. The rock slipped and gave way. His knee banged against the rock wall, his foot forced down violently, jangling in the air, weightless. *I'm falling. I'm dead.*

But he did not fall. He clutched even harder to the rock wall, clenching it, hugging it—and held on. And within the flow of that single motion, a remarkable thing happened: his face also reached closer to the rock and kissed it—in farewell or in thankfulness, I cannot say. It was a pure bodily reaction, yet it was sacred; it was an act of instinctive reverence. He was kissing his fate, kissing God, kissing nature, kissing the desert, kissing the moment, kissing the particular piece of rock that held his life and chose to spare him.

He continued moving left. Once again he lost a hold and thought he was dead. But again, he managed to hold on. Finally, he reached the edge of the outcropped rock. One last pivot and, throwing his weight over, he had it straddled. He held on for a moment, breathing. *I'm safe. I'm going to be okay.* He rolled over to the other side, clambered down the side slope, grabbed his backpack, and headed down the mountain.

He didn't bother to get out the flashlight. He was burning lucid, white hot. He pounded down the gully, invincible. Through the dark, his feet sensed every rock. His body was a beautiful machine; it moved with certainty, almost with an uncanny foreknowledge. He knew at each turn what he would find. He was flush, fierce, bewildered with his own reality, his own natural power. He felt like a warrior, welcome in the desert.

———————

According to a glossary entry nearly omitted from the final manuscript, the inner corpse is "a figurative device representing the living presence of death in the unconscious mind." Though an intellectual elaboration of Brother Void's visceral insights on the cliff and in subsequent encounters, the phrase "inner corpse" was initially designed to shock and amuse.

Viewed as an archeological artifact, the phrase traces Brother Void's journey from dark humor to dark truth-telling. In the venerable "crazy wisdom" tradition of the laughing monk, he initially envisioned the inner corpse as the dark, twisted cousin of the inner child, a figure common in pop-psych literature. Yet, even in this earliest incarnation, a deeper truth lay at its core, its invention driven by a need to honor the darker half of the spirit and affirmed in the work of other thinkers and seekers, including Ernest Becker in his pivotal work, *Denial of Death:*

The idea of death, the fear of it, haunts the human animal like nothing else; it is a mainspring of human activity—activity designed largely to avoid the fatality of death, to overcome it by denying in some way that it is the ultimate destiny for man.

On the cliff, this denial of death was operating in concentrated form. When Brother Void first grasped the danger he was in, his denial was so strong that it overruled, for a time, even his survival instinct. He had very limited strength in his fingers and legs, and yet he wasted valuable time pretending that he wasn't really there, that it wasn't really happening. Becker would argue that we live this way all the time. Intellectually, we acknowledge that death happens, but we pretend it won't ever happen to us. Such elaborate denial fundamentally shapes our life and character. The overwhelming sense of death is still there, buried deep in our unconscious. This is the inner corpse, and we dedicate a vast array of psychic resources to keep it invisible and to suppress it. When Brother Void gathered his courage on the cliff and made his move, it was a profound acknowledgment of reality. He faced death—and his denial of death—and chose to act.

———————

To survive over the long run, a mystic must learn to voyage inward without dangling off a cliff face. Mystics traditionally sit in silent contemplation or wander the countryside muttering in paradox. They tend to speak obliquely of a larger reality, something deeper and more encompassing than the inner corpse.

After emerging from his valley of death, Brother Void too would encounter a larger reality, one that he came to call the Void and from which he later took his own name. His spiritual discipline at that time was working in a rib joint. As a self-imposed penance and ministry, he was organizing in his community for more affordable housing. His daily meditation consisted of reading Alan Watts, Nietzsche, Marx, Camus, Paul Tillich, and others.

One hot summer night, after a strenuous and lengthy period of reading, he stood up, stretched, and walked out onto the outdoor terrace of his apartment, fourteen stories above New York City. He was leaning against the railing, looking out across the city, looking out at the building across the way. He was staring intently at this building, trying to fathom it—it an object in the world, he perceiving it. And without smoking anything, he reached a moment when he could not distinguish the building from his own perception of it or from himself. And suddenly, the ground under his feet became empty and the bottom of whomever he was fell away. He was pitched into a vast, dark, endless, evaporating space. There was no longer any foundation underfoot, nothing solid, nothing given, nothing at all. Into this yawning emptiness he was falling, falling downward sickeningly into nothing, falling outward in all directions without limit.

Eternity was gazing through him, a terrible immensity annihilating him, demanding his surrender, and yet, in some strange way, requiring him for its own integrity. He was neither dead nor dying, yet he felt as if he had been put to death. He could feel that death lived in him—and always had—as real and alive and powerful as life.

His whole life seemed a lie, an elaborate sleight of hand. Every aspect of his personality was little more than a blind slab of psychic armor, a false self, a pretension, a self-deluding vanity. Paradoxically, seeing himself this way felt like the first true moment in his life.

He was being summoned. He was being called to embrace the terrifying Otherness all around him; embrace the world's horrors and hopelessness; embrace all that he feared and all that he had ever pushed away. He was being asked to be perfect, to be holy; to become a saint, a superman; to become as infinite as the moment, as omniscient as the gaze upon him, as selfless as God.

He had nothing to offer but love. Only love could open him. Only an absolute, selfless love of all things for all time could empty him enough to meet and match the ferocity of the gaze upon him. As if in challenge, the image of an old Chinese woman he had seen on the street several days before came into his mind. Her face was pockmarked; her hands, warped. She was hunched over, unpleasant and prickly. Even now, as she was called to mind, he found her contrary and repulsive. But he had to open up to her or be crushed.

Before this final denouement could play itself out, the vision abruptly ended. There he was, still standing on the terrace, hands still holding on to the railing, the building across the way still there, just as before.

In the days and years that followed, Brother Void struggled to reconcile his vision of the Void with the life he was leading. He made it the nickname of his monastic retreat, a group house he shared for a while in a Boston neighborhood, emblazoned on a cardboard sign that slowly grew warped by the rain. He tried to tell his friends about what had happened but there wasn't a story he could really tell. "You are our gateway to the Void," they said. "Every group of friends should have one." Was he being humored or honored? He didn't know. His activist work in the community alternated between periods of tremendous energy and focus, and periods of lassitude brought on by doubts and philosophical uncertainties that had been kicked up by the Void.

My epistemology, ontology, and teleology are all shot to hell, he wrote. *What am I supposed to do with my loosely Marxist worldview, now that I have experienced Infinity? What is the point of any historical project to end injustice, if Time is an Eternal Now, and suffering and surrender are a necessary part of some deeper reality?* And how could he continue to believe that reality was socially constructed, or mediated by language, when he had experienced what felt like an absolute revelation outside of any text?

How was Brother Void, an atheist, even supposed to know whether he had experienced God? And if it was God, *Now what?* he wondered. Was he supposed to grow his beard and join a yeshiva in New Jersey? Or shave his head and dance around in airports? What if a religious person had had the same experience? There were no angels, or fat little cherubim with trumpets, or severe blue-skinned gods with arms to spare. There was nothing even blissful about it. In fact, it was the most disturbing, viscerally unpleasant, gut-wrenchingly apocalyptic experience of his life. If a religious person had gone through this, would she have recognized God at all? Would it have shaken her faith, the same way it had shaken his doubts? Or was the Void an atheist's version of God? Would a true believer have had a very different experience, one filled with the proper meanings and images of her faith? His journals are filled with such reflections.

But the Void refused to be confined to moments of reflection. It continued to wash over Brother Void at unexpected times and in unexpected places. One evening, after a long walk, he and I lay down in a wide open field under the blossoming night sky. It was then, he told me later, lying there in the field, damp grass under his shoulder blades, dark space boundless and raw above him, that it happened again.

He was afraid to think. His ideas could no longer hold the scale of the things they called forth. He wanted life to be simple again: to be dazzled by the night sky, not assaulted by heart-rending awe. But there was no place left in him for mild wonder. Something had been pried open—would it ever close back over and let him be?

It continued like this, until one night. It was late, he was lying awake in bed. He was trying to quiet his mind but he could not. It was coming again. The dread. The icy fingers stripping away the walls. The panic; his heart clutching at air. It was strong this time. He sat up. *Face it now,* he thought. *Don't shake it, don't turn away, don't hide, don't pretend. This time, face it. But what is happening? Just face it.* It was coming now, fierce. He crossed his legs under him, straightened his back. And then it came. The fabric of the air gave way. An immense field of horror spread before him. And from within him a terrible emptiness rose to meet it, hemorrhaging through the room, into the night, to the zeniths of space and time. *Now go, go, go. Don't turn away. Go through it, follow it, sail right on into it.* And he dove forward like a reckless cone of life, leaving behind all he had ever known or wished for.

———————

It is impossible to really know what happened to Brother Void in this final encounter. The mystical state of consciousness is a state of knowledge experienced as a state of feeling. This paradox, as William James understood well, makes reporting near impossible:

> No one can make clear to another who has never had a certain feeling, in what the quality or worth of it consists. One must have musical ears to know the value of a symphony; one must have been in love one's self to understand a lover's state of mind. Lacking the heart or ear, we cannot interpret the musician or the lover justly,

and are even likely to consider him weak-minded or absurd. The mystic finds that most of us accord to his experiences an equally incompetent treatment.

When I press Brother Void, he describes only the psychological sequence of events. He did face "it," he says, though he declines to elaborate on what "it" was. On that night he found the courage to acknowledge its truth and power, to let go of his fear, let go of his wish to continue to be who he thought he was, and let go of how he had always imagined the world to be. He welcomed it, and as he sailed on into it, he felt his whole self being burned away. After many moments like this, he passed some threshold, finally piercing the sphere of terror. He became rooted in stillness, his spine like a lightning rod in the earth, and wave upon wave of energy blew out from him, drenching the room. *You cannot understand. Every pore was wide open. It was as if my soul and my whole body had been turned inside out. I was facing the world for the first time.*

Brother Void presides over his own church now. The Book of Daily Afflictions is complete. Every time I read it, I imagine Brother Void deep in thought, waiting alone for the congregation to gather, struggling to bind his heart anew to the sacred words of the text.

the book of daily afflictions
the book of daily afflictions
the book of daily afflictions
the book of daily afflictions
the book of daily afflictions
the book of daily afflictions
the book of daily afflictions
the book of daily afflictions
the book of daily afflictions
the book of daily afflictions
the book of daily afflictions
the book of daily afflictions
the book of daily afflictions
the book of daily afflictions
the book of daily afflictions
the book of daily afflictions
the book of daily afflictions
the book of daily afflictions
the book of daily afflictions
the book of daily afflictions
the book of daily afflictions
the book of daily afflictions
the book of daily afflictions
the book of daily afflictions
the book of daily afflictions
the book of daily afflictions
the book of daily afflictions
the book of daily afflictions
the book of daily afflictions
the book of daily afflictions
the book of daily afflictions
the book of daily afflictions
the book of daily afflictions
the book of daily afflictions

life
life
life
life
life
life
life
life
life
life
life
life
life
life
life
life
life
life
life
life
life
life
life
life
life
life
life
life
life
life
life
life

LIFE BREAKS EVERYONE,
BUT SOME ARE STRONG
IN THE BROKEN PLACES.

—Ernest Hemingway

THE INTERSTATE OF LIFE

You are free and that is why you are lost.
—FRANZ KAFKA

On the interstate of life you rarely reach your destination. In rest stop after rest stop, you look for signs of God, or happiness, or just reason enough to get back on the road. But is it not right and fitting that you lose your way? Isn't such failure itself evidence of the sublime? Granted, the bleary-eyed, caffeine-dazed monotony of the interstate of life may often feel like an endless bad dream. But the roadside wreckage that marks your journey—the discarded quarts of oil, the busted hubcaps, the insect bodies splattered on your windshield, the coffee lids scattered at your feet—aren't these signs that, in a certain way, you have already arrived?

It's not whether I arrive; it's how I lose my way.

LIVING A WORTHLESS LIFE

Whoever despises himself still respects himself as one who despises.
—FRIEDRICH NIETZSCHE

When you are unhappy, you find yourself prone to feelings of envy and jealousy. When your own life seems worthless, you often look at someone else's life and want it for yourself. But remember, however much you might want his car, career, lover, or even good looks or intelligence, you would never, given the chance, choose to be that person. You would never choose to exchange souls, because your ego is fiercely bound to your defects and failings no matter how appalling they may be. Once you realize this—once you realize that no matter how worthless your life is, it's still the only one you would ever choose to have—you can begin to see yourself with new eyes.

My life is worthless, but it is mine.

BEING THERE THEN

Life must be lived forwards, however, it can only be
understood backwards.
—SØREN KIERKEGAARD

You can understand your life only after it happens. Unfortunately, by
then it's too late. The previous moment is already gone and the
present moment is again incomprehensible. If you are to embrace
your life as an evolving whole, you must think of yourself as a
story—admittedly, a highly biased and poorly researched pulp
paperback that is constantly being revised and incrementally updat-
ed with no sign of when it will end or what the characters will do
next, yet a story that is uniquely yours. Seeing yourself as a story
helps you reconcile your forward motion and your backward gaze.
It gives you hope that, at the very end, it will all somehow make
sense, even if you break off in mid-sentence.

I will understand my life perfectly once it is over.

THE SUPERMARKET OF LIFE

As a man's real power grows and his knowledge widens, ever the way he can follow grows narrower: until at last he chooses nothing, but does only and wholly what he must do.
—URSULA LE GUIN

In the supermarket of life you can choose your religion like toothpaste; you can test-drive spouses before you buy. You can go anywhere, be anyone, consume anything. Giddy with the possibilities, you fill your shopping cart to the brim. But a time comes when the sheer quantity of choice leaves you numb. You ache for something deeper and more potent, something you cannot find on the shelves. Slowly, item by item—extra-soft, reduced-fat, double-ply, and super-chunky—you must empty your cart. With nothing chosen, your conscience, visions, and gods can now choose you, until at last—your cart empty and your heart set free by a single burning necessity—you breeze past the other shoppers stuck in the checkout lane of life, and head for the door.

I choose to be chosen.

LIVING AS A WORK OF ART

The stupid believe that to be truthful is easy; only the artist, the great artist, knows how difficult it is.
—WILLA CATHER

Many of us imagine living as a work of art, but few consider the difficulties. First, you must dig down deep to where your inner artist lies trapped in a spirit-crushing day job. Having unearthed your unruly visions, you must then be willing to suffer for them. You must consent to be a rough draft much of the time. You must be prepared to destroy yourself in order to create yourself anew. You must revel in the hardness of your hammer, showing no pity to the forsaken shards littering the drop-cloth of your life. Finally, having offered yourself up as the willing clay of your own imagination, you must note, with some chagrin, that your inner artist is a drunken, moody son-of-a-bitch.

I am a difficult canvas.

KEEPING TO THE DARK PATH

What is meant by light? To gaze with undimmed eyes on all darkness.
—NIKOS KAZANTZAKIS

On the dark and difficult path you have chosen, you sometimes lose your way. Your spirit becomes suffused in a warm, fuzzy light. The Universe becomes infinitely benevolent. Things start to happen for a reason. Eventually you hit bottom and purchase the collected works of Yanni. But do not be fooled. Remember, there are two kinds of light: the steady blue flame at the heart of darkness and the false, desperate sunshine of the cheery countenance. Your wisdom will grow not by conjuring figures of light, but by making the darkness conscious. So pick up the path you lost and, once again, be on your dark and difficult way.

The dark path lights my way.

self
self
self
self
self
self
self
self
self
self
self
self
self
self
self
self
self
self
self
self
self
self
self
self
self
self
self
self
self
self
self
self
self
self
self

THE UNCONSCIOUS WANTS
TRUTH. IT CEASES TO SPEAK
TO THOSE WHO WANT
SOMETHING ELSE MORE
THAN TRUTH.

—Adrienne Rich

DEEPENING THE CRISIS

If you're going through hell, keep going.
—WINSTON CHURCHILL

Meaningful personal growth rarely occurs without anguish, crisis, and loss. Maybe you're in a dead-end relationship or haven't come out to your parents. Or maybe you've got a secure job but always wanted to make it on your own. You need to change your life. But you're not going to make a move until things get a lot worse. In such a state, the only way forward is deeper into crisis.

Pushing yourself deliberately into crisis is never easy. After all, it's only natural to resist permanent damage to your identity. But if you can bludgeon your resistance into submission, you can reach the point of no return. Past this point, you are fully committed to the crisis. With no way back, your once-idle doubts and speculations must crystallize into desperate convictions. With your consciousness polarized into a brawl of warring factions, your choices will at last lie clearly and unforgivingly before you.

The deeper my crisis, the clearer my choices.

LISTENING TO YOUR INNER CRITIC

Anxiety is the essential condition of intellectual and artistic creation
and everything that is finest in human history.
—CHARLES FRANKEL

We all know that insidious voice that visits when we're trying to
write or paint or just get our life together, the one that cuts us down
before we begin, the one that says we'll never be good enough.
You're told that if only you can push this voice aside, your best, most
natural self will flow freely out of you and into the task at hand. This
might be the right approach when you're truly paralyzed. But is it
not better to steel yourself for the worst and listen carefully to what
your inner critic is actually trying to say? "You're full of shit. You're
lying to yourself, and you know it. You haven't decided which rules
to break and which to follow. You're using too much blue again."

Your inner critic is a vital part of who you are. Who else knows
you so well? Who else can offer such fine-grained criticism, as well
as finger your most cunning strategies of self-delusion and sabotage?
Such a rich heritage of self-knowledge should be channeled toward

self-improvement. Instead of blocking out your inner critic, why not use it to burn away all your dross and second-rate pretensions?

I am my own best critic.

SELFLESS SELFISHNESS

Why are you unhappy? Because 99.9% of everything you do is for yourself—and there isn't one.
—WEI WU WEI

We all wish for happiness, some of us desperately. Yet few of us find it. Even after you score that cushy job, or have that perfect wedding, or get that liver spot surgically removed, you are likely to remain unhappy. Only after years of disappointment do you finally learn that happiness cannot be pursued; it can only emerge as the result of some deeper calling. Being happy requires the rarest of things: to want something more than your own happiness. To lose yourself in a task, to squander yourself for a purpose, to surrender to love— these are the things that make you truly happy. Even the most self-obsessed egomaniacs must give of themselves to advance their own fat-headed self-actualization. In life, as in love, it's only through a self-less act of devotion that your most selfish longings are fulfilled.

Selfishly, I give of myself.

THE NAUSEA OF LANGUAGE—
A GUIDED EXERCISE

Only the hand that erases can write the true thing.
—MEISTER ECKHART

Sometimes you feel caught in a web of language, your identity defined by words you never chose and cannot seem to shake. Whatever the words—hysteric, geek, slut, atheist, gen-X-er, Hispanic, or temporary departmental associate project assistant— they work their way insidiously into the story you tell about yourself. To break free and rewrite your own story, you must first get in touch with the nausea at the heart of language. You can do this in the quiet of your own home, by following a few simple steps.

Select the word that most binds your identity. With pen and paper, write it out in big block letters. Now, focus your eyes on the word you have written down and gently consider its claims upon you. At first, you may not notice any change. Remain focused. In time, the letters before you begin to swim. The word relinquishes all authority. It seems alien, its spelling almost random. With sickening speed, a chain reaction spreads through the whole language until its arbitrary structure stretches out before you, raw and meaningless.

At this point, your own personal narrative, the text that is you, may begin to hemorrhage in big, wet chunks. The nausea of language is upon you.

I am the text that I erase.

THE USES OF OBSESSION

It is surely a great calamity for a human being to have no obsessions.
—ROBERT BLY

If you take a balanced, healthy approach to the multiple claims on your life—to family, friends, love, community, and work—you may feel grounded and well respected, but your deepest longings will inevitably suffer. The singular visions plaguing your imagination may never make it onto the page, screen, or stage. So you are faced with a great and difficult choice, one that men and women throughout the ages have had to face: repression or obsession? Do you stamp out your feverish dreams and return all your phone calls? Or do you open the gates to your neurotic desires, mount your obsessions and wildly ride them where they must carry you, trampling over life's sweet comforts?

> When obsessed, I accomplish great things; when repressed,
> I follow through on important commitments.

OPENING UP
TO YOUR INNER PSYCHOPATH

A man needs a little madness or else he never dares to cut the rope
and be free.
—NIKOS KAZANTZAKIS

Inside each of us is an inner psychopath waiting for the right
moment to explode. All of us can remember such moments. You
step into a crowded elevator. The eyes of another passenger find
your own and flick away. The doors close. You find yourself
enveloped in the stale mouthwash of social convention. Each person is silent and rigid, facing forward, intently watching the panel
of illuminated numbers as they flicker from floor to floor. As the
silence thickens, you are drawn to a secret part of yourself that
itches for release, that swells with the desire for rupture: your inner
psychopath.

When you open up to your inner psychopath, you step into a
new dimension of personal freedom. Turning to face your fellow
passengers, you might say, "We never talk. Don't you think it's time
we had a talk? I think it is. So listen up. Yo, losers, look at me, and listen the fuck up! All right? Do you fuckin' get it, or what? Can't you
see what's happening here? Make some human fuckin' contact, for

chrissakes. You! Yeah, you. Say hello, real nice. Now you. Nice and easy, buddy. No fast moves, or it's sweet bye bye. That's good, real good. We're not fuckin' robots, you know! We're free, self-realizing, social fuckin' organisms! Okay? So let's start acting like it, goddammit! All right, I feel better, don't you? I know you do." By sharing with others in this way, you honor the many voices held within you. By staying open to your inner psychopath, you keep the rest of your personality on its toes.

I'm not insane, but parts of me are.

FINDING SORROW

Let my hidden weeping arise and blossom.
—RAINER MARIA RILKE

When you get depressed, it's comforting to remember that deep inside you is a well of pain. This pain can help you. It's a reservoir of self-knowledge and nourishment. When you're able to welcome this pain, it can carry you out of depression into sorrow.

When depressed, you are merely numb and listless. But in sorrow, you feel the fine-grained texture of loss. Whereas depression diminishes your world, sorrow teaches you the true value of the things you mourn. Sorrow is the other side of joy—a dark, moist cradle of grief that slowly nourishes you, a solemn vigil that honors what you love. So the next time you are ensnared in darkness, cut through the gray armor of depression straight to the dark heart of sorrow.

Lost in depression, I am found in sorrow.

THE SUBURB WITHIN

You must proceed there, that way, where today you are least at home.
—FRIEDRICH NIETZSCHE

Most of us think of suburbia as a physical place. A place where folks value comfort, safety, and a good electric Saran Wrap cutter. A place where you can boldly assert your independence from cultural enrichment. But suburbia also exists within us. You might live in the middle of a big city, but there could still be a white picket fence around your imagination. You can take the subway to work but still park your identity in a two-car garage. This is inner suburbia, and you probably moved here long ago. You've let yourself be shaped by your fears of the unknown. You've learned to contain your longings and sympathies within a comfortable zone, measured and mediocre. To grow, you must move toward otherness. You must quit the ranch house of your soul and head for the forbidden places—your inner wilderness, inner bohemia, or even your inner inner city. The answers you need lie there, where you are least at home.

I must quit the ranch house of my soul.

family
family
family
family
family
family
family
family
family
family
family
family
family
family
family
family
family
family
family
family
family
family
family
family
family
family
family
family
family
family

FAMILIES . . . ARE MAGNETS
THAT BOTH HOLD US CLOSE
AND DRIVE US AWAY.

—George Howe Colt

EMBRACING THE LIFE FORCED UPON YOU

Freedom is what you do with what's been done to you.
—JEAN-PAUL SARTRE

From the beginning you are the victim of circumstance. You're born, kicking and screaming, into an unknown family. As a child, you soak up influences that mold your mind in certain ways. When you finally get a driver's license and move out of the house, you think you're free—but you marry someone who looks like your mother and drinks like your father. By the time you figure out who you are or what you want, a life has already been forced upon you. But it's never too late to change. Although you can't begin again from scratch, you can make a splendid ragout from the mishmash of damaged goods in your cupboard.

I choose how to live a life I didn't choose.

THE NURTURING POWER
OF DYSFUNCTIONAL FAMILIES

Happy families are all alike; every unhappy family is unhappy in its own
way.
—LEO TOLSTOY

It is important, if you grew up in a dysfunctional family, to take time
to reflect on the competitive edge it has given you. People from
happy, harmonious homes may feel healthy and well adjusted, but
they're fixed on one family model, which they try to emulate the
rest of their lives. If you grew up in a dysfunctional family, however,
you may be deeply damaged, but you've acquired a broad reper-
toire of negative models to outgrow. As you go about your adult life,
you should thank your parents: they have given you the kind of edu-
cation that happy children, through no fault of their own, never
receive.

My parents taught me everything I need to unlearn.

THE BOOT CAMP OF LIFE .

> We delude ourselves that we want to imbue our children with honesty;
> instead what we want is to imbue them with our particular form of
> dishonesty.
> —SIDNEY HARRIS

Some of us are so damaged by our dysfunctional childhoods that we cannot unlearn everything our parents taught us. When this happens, you must make your dysfunction work for you. A good way to begin is to remember that your family is a boot camp designed just for you. In the heat of battle every brutality and indignity that soldiers have suffered in boot camp becomes an immediate reflex that helps them fight, kill, and survive. This is how you should feel about your family. As you move out into the adult jungle, you're prepared for battle. Not only are you ready on a hair-trigger to detonate a flexible array of adult issues, but you've been rigorously trained to handle the operational systems of adult institutions, including passive aggression in the school system, guilt bartering in organized religion, and domination-submission patterns between corporations and government.

As you look back on your unhappy childhood, you realize that your dysfunctional family has prepared you to survive in a dysfunctional world.

Thanks to my dysfunctional childhood, I'm ready to kick some adult ass.

LIVING THE UNLIVED LIFE

Nothing has a stronger influence ... on ... children, than the unlived
life of the parent.
—CARL JUNG

Some of us have children too early in life. Invariably, we lay our
thwarted dreams and toxic disappointments upon their heads, hoping they will live the life we neglected to live. The rest of us figure,
why not have our life first and then have the kids? We soon find,
however, that this is not so easy. As the world grows more complex
and the possibilities for experiencing things multiply, it becomes ever
more difficult to work in enough living before the close of our
baby-making years. Eventually, you realize that the only way to beat
the clock is to live your life as furiously as possible—which means
starting earlier, moving faster, and holding out longer. You've got to
crank through travel fantasies, fringe lifestyles, multiple careers,
extreme sports, and designer drugs and gorge yourself on liquor
and sex as fast and as hard as you can. How else can you expect to
get over yourself enough to really be there for your kids when it
counts? So the next time you find yourself power partying, remem-

ber to ratchet it up another notch because only when you live your unlived life will your children be free to live theirs.

I binge for my kids.

THE HEALING POWER
OF SICK PARENTS

When the father gives to his son, both laugh; when the son gives to his father, both cry.
—YIDDISH PROVERB

There is much that can keep a family apart, but there's nothing that brings them together like sickness and death. Whether you have grown estranged from your parents or just find yourself too busy to spend time with them, sickness can heal this separation. It's certainly a tragedy when parents fall grievously ill or slowly grow less able to take care of themselves. But it is also a great and unique opportunity to strengthen your relationship with them, and you must seize it. No matter how busy you are, no matter how much resentment you feel, you must go to them and be with them. As their powers decline, your love may find surprising new space to grow into. When they can no longer feed themselves, you can do it for them, as they once did for you. When they can no longer bathe and wipe themselves, it's now you who changes their diapers. Sickness can force an intimacy that both parent and child have longed for.

Sickness and death bring me closer to my parents.

love
love
love
love
love
love
love
love
love
love
love
love
love
love
love
love
love
love
love
love
love
love
love
love
love
love
love
love
love
love
love
love

LOVE IS THE EXTREMELY
DIFFICULT REALIZATION
THAT SOMEONE OTHER
THAN ONESELF IS REAL.

—Iris Murdoch

THE OTHER SIDE OF LOVE

I love her and she loves me and together we hate each other with a
wild hatred born of love.
—J. AUGUST STRINDBERG

When you truly love another with all your heart, you lay the foundations for pain, rage, and devastation. When you place your heart
in the hands of your beloved, it may come back to you: a blood
pump in a pickle jar. When this happens, you cross to the other side
of love. Each shared secret becomes a twisted barb. As tenderly as
you once surrendered, you now rage with fury and hopelessness.
The sweeter your loving, the more exacting your bitterness. As you
cross from one side of love to the other, you are learning to accept
that agony follows bliss as surely as night follows day.

The bliss I feel now is sweet with the agony that is sure to follow.

PASSION AND COMPANIONSHIP

Love creates tension; sex relieves it.
—WOODY ALLEN

We all want to have warm companionship and hot sex with the person we love. However, this is not often possible. With one lover you might feel so familiar that there's almost no friction, tension, or sex. With another you might enjoy emotionally supercharged sex simply because there's no other effective way to communicate.

Must you always choose between passion and companionship? If so, passion would seem the obvious choice, since you are permitted to go outside the bonds of marriage for a good conversation but not for a good fuck. Then again, it's hard to stomach the idea of spending forty years with a hot number who doesn't share your fascination with Wittgenstein. If you're unable to face these trade-offs, then you must keep seeking, hoping that in a dark corner of the next singles bar you'll find the one perfectly companionable intellectual nymphomaniac.

Unwilling to settle for passionate misunderstanding or
frigid companionship, I am alone.

LOVING THE WRONG PERSON

Let our scars fall in love.
—GALWAY KINNELL

We're all seeking that special person who is right for us. But if you've been through enough relationships, you begin to suspect there's no right person, just different flavors of wrong. Why is this? Because you yourself are wrong in some way, and you seek out partners who are wrong in some complementary way. But it takes a lot of living to grow fully into your own wrongness. It isn't until you finally run up against your deepest demons, your unsolvable problems—the ones that make you truly who you are—that you're ready to find a life-long mate. Only then do you finally know what you're looking for. You're looking for the wrong person. But not just any wrong person: the *right* wrong person—someone you lovingly gaze upon and think, "This is the problem I want to have."

> I will find that special person who is wrong for me in
> just the right way.

FUCKED BY LOVE

It takes a nail to drive out a nail.
—SALVADORAN PROVERB

When you have loved and lost, you are fucked. You don't want to begin a new relationship because how could you possibly love another? You don't want a fling because in the shadow of real love, what would be the point? You don't want to be alone because it hurts too much. You can't be with the one you lost because he or she is either dead or sleeping with someone else. With no real options left, you balm your pain with fantasy and memory. You lie alone in bed, haunted by the tingle of phantom limbs. When the rebound relationship comes along, you may be sleeping with someone new—but you're making love to the ghost of the one you lost.

Finally, you must face the truth. The only way to cast out your ghost is to fall hard for someone new—someone who might hurt you even more deeply. In this way, you heal your broken heart, preparing it to again be broken.

I must find someone who can hurt me more deeply.

SEEING THINGS THROUGH TO TOTAL CATASTROPHE

Inspired by the absolute hopelessness of everything, I felt relieved, as if a great burden had been lifted from my shoulders.
—HENRY MILLER

When you look back on a failed relationship, you often wonder how it could have gone on for so long. For months you knew it wasn't working. Why didn't you get out before it became an irrevocable disaster? The answer is simple: Because it needed to end in catastrophe. You needed to poison the well and bludgeon your heart beyond repair. You needed to exhaust all your reserves. Anything less, and you'd still be holding out hope. You can always muddle along from minor disaster to minor disaster, but it takes truly heroic stamina to see things through to total catastrophe.

It's a catastrophe, but it's the one I need.

BREAKING UP WITH YOURSELF

The majority of people are subjective toward themselves and objective toward all others . . . but the real task is, in fact, to be objective toward oneself and subjective toward all others.
—SØREN KIERKEGAARD

The time immediately after a bad relationship is filled with promise. It's as if you've rid yourself of something that was weighing you down and keeping you from reaching your full potential. You feel light and clear and free. But this honeymoon with yourself is short-lived and you're soon in a new relationship fraught with the same old problems. This pattern continues until you finally realize that most of the issues are your own, and that to be truly free, you must break up with yourself.

Doing so is not always easy. You might become nostalgic for the better times you've had with yourself and feel sad to let yourself go. But you must be strong. You must remember the pain and anguish done to you and be ruthless. You must look yourself in the eye and say all those things you've been keeping inside for years. You must dump yourself without remorse or apology, and as you slowly get over yourself, you mustn't call.

I can be my own best ex.

career
career
career
career
career
career
career
career
career
career
career
career
career
career
career
career
career
career
career
career
career
career
career
career
career
career
career
career
career
career

EVERYONE HAS TALENT.
WHAT IS RARE IS THE
COURAGE TO FOLLOW
THAT "TALENT" TO THE
DARK PLACE WHERE IT
LEADS.

—Erica Jong

FAILING AT WHAT MATTERS

We must learn to regard people less in the light of what they do or
don't do, and more in the light of what they suffer.
—DIETRICH BONHOEFFER

As you watch TV or gaze up the corporate ladder, everyone but you
seems accomplished and successful. How sweet it is, then, to realize
that failure is what life is all about; failure is why you're here. Isn't
there more nobility in your failed attempt to conquer your self, or
to relieve the solitude of the one you love, or to just continue living
this difficult life in the face of oncoming death than there is in the
greatest success of any banker, brain surgeon, or late-night aerobics
instructor? You can ultimately succeed only at unimportant things.
The loftiest things in life always end in failure. So the next time
you're suffering from low self-esteem, remember this: every beautiful, rich, successful person you see on TV will, like you, fail at what
matters to them most. If you seek something worthwhile, seek failure.

I fail at the most important things.

DOING THE WRONG THING

Make the right mistake.
—YOGI BERRA

There are times in life when you're lost and no job or career path feels right. You're doing something, but you're doing it half-hearted-ly. When you find yourself drifting and slacking like this, remember: you don't have to know what you're doing, you just have to do it as hard as you possibly can.

It's only when you do something with all your heart that you find out what it is you're really doing. When everything feels kind of wrong, you have to choose one wrong thing and work really hard at it. This will help you see your way clear to the next wrong thing, and the next, until you reach some right thing—if you ever do. Obviously, working hard at the wrong thing may result in irritability, depression, embezzlement, or industrial sabotage. But this is a small price to pay for finding your true life's work.

I don't know what I'm doing, but I'm doing it as hard as
I possibly can.

IN PURSUIT OF FAILURE

When your bow is broken and your last arrow spent, then shoot,
shoot with your whole heart.
—ZEN ADAGE

When you consider failure, it is important to distinguish between
two kinds. There is the failure of giving up, turning around, and walk-
ing away. Although this failure holds a certain seductive appeal, you
must not let it divert you from the true heart of failure: the tri-
umphant defeat of all your hopes, stratagems, and efforts. This is the
ultimate failure that tells you who you are. You want failure you have
to work hard for, failure you put everything into—failure so rich
with loss and pain that, even years later, it gives you the basis from
which to make yourself anew, the scar tissue that deeply confirms
your aliveness. Real failure requires real effort and is its own reward.

A thing worth failing is worth failing well.

THE HAVOC OF SATURN'S RETURN

The ideal must get real: this is the tragedy of youth.
—G. W. F. HEGEL (*paraphrase*)

It is difficult to live on the edge and also remain meaningfully employed. No matter how much you burn and shine at the beginning of each career move, within a short while you lose your spark, your drive, and your health benefits. You feel deeply hurt that no employer will pay you to stagger forward willfully along the dark path that you alone must travel. Finally, after years of this manic casting about for meaning, you realize that, all the while you've been changing jobs, what you've really needed to do is change yourself. This simple, elegant insight throws you into a deep depression. An eerie quiet descends upon you. Held in a cosmic trance, you look up into the night sky and observe with dismay that the planet Saturn—that bloated sign of order and disorder—has returned to the same place it was when you were born 29.6 years ago. Even though you don't believe in astrology, you somehow slide deeper into depression.

It may take years, but as you shed your youthful illusions and learn to take yourself more seriously, you finally emerge from your dark time of reckoning. You're now stronger and more free because astrology has taught you one important lesson: it will be another 29.6 years before you feel this bad again.

Every 29.6 years a large planet will mess up my life.

SUCCEEDING AT FAILURE

Success is the ability to go from failure to failure with no loss of
enthusiasm.
—WINSTON CHURCHILL

We often think of failure in a negative light. But if you adopt the right
attitude, you can make failure a constant and loyal friend, the one
thing you can count on in a shifting, fickle world. If you can learn to
experience the bitter taste of defeat at the very moment you com-
mit yourself to a new project, what more can go wrong? Such a
preemptive approach to failure can save both time and heartache.
Another helpful approach is to see failure as a great teacher. In this
light, a broken career is actually a rich compost of defeated experi-
ments; success, a progression of failures that leads you somewhere.
Finally, you can treat failure as your true life's work. Great artists have
always known that the secret of fulfillment is to have a task you can
devote your entire life to—but to sustain you, it must be something
you cannot possibly do.

When failure is my goal, I cannot fail.

THE TRAGEDY OF COMMITMENT

Whoever wants something great must be able to limit himself.
—WOLFGANG VON GOETHE

Sometimes you are paralyzed with indecision. You can't bring your-self to choose any one future because to choose one is to forsake the promise of all others. Yet not choosing is making you crazy. In such a state, drastic action is necessary. You must choose—and then, one by one, murder all the futures you passed over. Like a faithful companion you've cherished all through your youth, you must lead each future back behind the shed, and even if it looks up at you with those big eyes, dreamy with possibility, you must put the cold muz-zle to its head and pull the trigger. You must do it, again and again, for each future that competes for the attentions of your heart. Only then are you ready for commitment. Only then can you pursue the one thing which will, in time and after much mourning, become all things to you.

The future is full of possibilities that I must shoot in the head.

politics
politics
politics
politics
politics
politics
politics
politics
politics
politics
politics
politics
politics
politics
politics
politics
politics
politics
politics
politics
politics
politics
politics
politics
politics
politics
politics
politics
politics
politics

YOU CAN HOLD BACK
FROM THE SUFFERING OF
THE WORLD, YOU HAVE FREE
PERMISSION TO DO SO, AND
IT IS IN ACCORDANCE WITH
YOUR NATURE, BUT PERHAPS
THIS VERY HOLDING BACK IS
THE ONE SUFFERING YOU
COULD HAVE AVOIDED.

—Franz Kafka

VISUALIZING THE WORST POSSIBLE WORLD—A GUIDED MEDITATION

Learn to hate your enemy well.
—JOHN HEARTFIELD

Many of us are alienated from politics. It seems like a big ugly mess and you wonder why you should care. When you're feeling this way, it can help to visualize the worst possible world.

Identify the politician who represents the extreme opposite of what you believe. Now use your imagination to transform the world according to his agenda. Acknowledge any stunned disgust or violent repulsion that arises. Imagine your loved ones caught in such a nightmare. Deepen and accelerate these feelings until the full horror of what could befall everything you cherish appears plainly before you. As you play out these monstrous visions of dystopia and apocalypse, cultivate a fine-grained hatred for the barbaric world your nemesis wishes to bring into being. Feel it seething around you, menacing you, as you wonder why you should care.

My enemy's monstrous visions remind me why politics matters.

THE INNER BIGOT

We contain the other, hopelessly and forever.
—JAMES BALDWIN

We live in a society scarred by hatred and misunderstanding. You look out at this world and figure that because you're not a church-burner, a gay-basher, or an officer of the LAPD, you're not a bigot. But inside each of us is an inner bigot waiting for things to get personal. Maybe you get iced out of a promotion, maybe Johnny's new teacher is gay, maybe your neighborhood is changing. That's when the inner bigot slithers into your throat and you hear yourself saying, "Those bastards are taking our jobs. Do what you want, but not near my children. Why do they all have to talk so loud? Can't you find a girl of your own kind? We moved to the suburbs for the schools."

Your inner bigot is the part of yourself you blame on others. It's how you flush out into the world the fear and self-hatred you refuse to take responsibility for. It's that exiled splinter of yourself you call niggerhomobitchpussykikewetbackwhitetrashfatfuck. To set things right, you must track it down. As you follow its treacherous movements and gather up what you have loosed upon others, you may also salvage the pieces that can make you whole.

I have met the Other and it is I.

COMPASSIONATE HYPOCRISY

You must be the change you want to see in the world.
—MOHANDAS GANDHI

You are not always strong enough to be the change you want to see in the world. This failing, however, should not lead you to abandon your efforts to help others. Instead, you must permit yourself a reasonable measure of hypocrisy. When it becomes too hard to fix yourself, you can still try to fix the world. When you feel miserable, let yourself reach out and connect with other people's misery. To make your own problems seem smaller and less onerous, you can always find some big global problem to take your pain away. As you set down your burdens and shoulder those of the world, draw strength from the knowledge that other people's problems are often easier to face than your own.

When I can't help myself, maybe someone else's
problems can help me.

BEING IN IT FOR YOURSELF

I don't do this work to change the world, I do it so the world doesn't change me.
—A. J. MUSTE (*paraphrase*)

Sometimes when you're involved in an idealistic crusade, you get wrapped up in your cause and lose perspective. If this happens, it's important to step back to better understand your motivations. Be honest with yourself: genocide, toxic sludge, and the AIDS epidemic are serious issues—but at a deeper level, they're opportunities for personal growth. Although it may seem that sacrifice in the name of a greater goal is noble and selfless, deep down it's really about egoism—in the best sense of the word. You're doing what you need to do to become who you want to be. In attempting to change the world, you're taking control of how the world changes you. So instead of laying self-righteous guilt trips on those who stay aloof and apathetic, admit that you're in this for yourself. Then, with a clear conscience, you can approach any of your cynical, self-absorbed friends and invite them to be in it for themselves too.

Toxic sludge can help me become a better person.

HOPELESSNESS CAN CHANGE THE WORLD

We are all incurables.
—ARCHBISHOP OSCAR ROMERO *(When asked why he was attending to the sick at a hospital for incurables)*

When you look around you, it is easy to feel hopeless. Things always seem to be getting worse, not better. Even those of us still working for a better tomorrow can have a bad day, week, or lifetime, when all seems lost. But such a lapse of faith should not be feared. On the contrary, you should welcome it as a revelation. Our situation *is* hopeless. Our cause *is* impossible.

You are faced with a stark choice: Do you dedicate yourself to an impossible cause? Or do you look after your own, making do as best you can? The choice is clear: You must dedicate yourself to an impossible cause. Why? Because we are all incurable. Because solidarity is a form of tenderness. Because the simple act of caring for the world is itself a victory. Take a stand—not because it will lead to anything, but because it is the right thing to do. We never know what can or can't be done; only what must be done.

I dedicate myself to an impossible cause.

philosophy
philosophy
philosophy
philosophy
philosophy
philosophy
philosophy
philosophy
philosophy
philosophy
philosophy
philosophy
philosophy
philosophy
philosophy
philosophy
philosophy
philosophy
philosophy
philosophy
philosophy
philosophy
philosophy
philosophy
philosophy
philosophy
philosophy
philosophy
philosophy
philosophy

EVERYTHING HAS BEEN
FIGURED OUT EXCEPT HOW
TO LIVE.

—Jean-Paul Sartre

THE PERILS OF CREATING YOUR OWN REALITY

Men make their own history but not in circumstances of their own
choosing.
—KARL MARX

It is often said that "you create your own reality." If you're a journal-
ist or a zookeeper, however, and you try to create your own reality,
you're likely to get fired or eaten. So we must be careful what we
mean. It's certainly true that your mental attitude can affect both
your experience of reality and your capacity to act on and change
the world around you. But does it follow that the Third World
children we see starving on TV are just bumming from their own
bad trip, and we're not responsible? Reality is a complex affair. Not
everyone has equal power to create his or her own reality. Nor can
we ignore the reality that is already there. As our approach to reality matures, we're learning that reality is really real after all, and we
cannot create it just as we please.

I create my own reality but it's not always the one I want.

FAITH AND IRONY

Having said clearly that it is no longer possible to speak innocently, [the ironist] will nonetheless have said what he wanted to say.
—UMBERTO ECO

We live in an age that has lost faith in itself. It is naive to care, gauche to be sincere, and downright suspicious to believe in a better tomorrow. But underneath your cool indifference you probably do care, although you distrust these feelings and you're ashamed to reveal them. Instead, you protect yourself with irony. Irony lets you off the hook and distances you from what you love. But irony also helps you negotiate your faithlessness. When you believe in something but also believe it's foolish to believe in anything, your only honest option is irony. It's how you pay lip service to your nihilism but also vaguely point beyond it.

To have faith today, you must at once affirm your faith and also ironically observe all that makes faith impossible. With one hand you must admit that it's all been done before, that everything is relative, that there's no ground for authenticity, and that every claim to truth is suspect. Then with the other hand, you can stake your claim with all your heart. In a faithless age irony is the only way to take yourself seriously, and the only way to show others that you distrust yourself enough for them to trust you.

Irony is the only way I can take myself seriously.

ONE STEP FROM OBLIVION

Things are entirely what they appear to be and *behind them* ... there is nothing.
—JEAN-PAUL SARTRE

Commercial air travel is a regular part of our lives, yet many of us still feel an eerie disquiet when we fly. You browse the in-flight magazines while a 37,000-foot chasm of emptiness lurks just beneath your shoes. You snack on little pretzels while a few inches away, life-sucking minus 60° airstreams whip by. The flight attendants point out exits that go nowhere.

In the air, as on the ground, behind every this or that lies all or nothing. This nothingness is papered over with illusion, habit, and little rituals, until something slices through the wrapper—until that moment when you hear the pilot's strained voice and feel your gut muscles clench. Will you grow huge enough to contain the hugeness of the moment? Or will you break apart in freakish panic?

In flight, as in life, you live one step from oblivion. You stand on nothing but your will. Your only security is to embrace insecurity. So the next time you fly, step on board as though entering a sacred battlefield, place your tray table in its upright and locked position, and stare straight past the pretzels and the chitchat into the jaws of the absolute.

The airline that doesn't kill me makes me stronger.

EVERYTHING HAPPENS
FOR A REASON

Mysteries are not necessarily miracles.
—GOETHE

Life is a confusing mess. You get blindsided by a drunk driver. You fall in love when you least expect to. Your firstborn becomes an accountant. Things happen that bring you great pain or pleasure and change your life forever. To find your bearings amid such chaos, you choose to believe that these events happen for a reason. It was meant to be, you tell yourself, and this comforts you. But to live truthfully, you must forgo this comfort. You must accept that there is no cosmic plan—just a story you tell yourself after the fact. As you try to weave each twist and turn of your life into some coherent whole, you artfully fashion the meaning you need. Things are not meant to be, they are made to mean.

Everything happens for a reason I make up.

religion
religion
religion
religion
religion
religion
religion
religion
religion
religion
religion
religion
religion
religion
religion
religion
religion
religion
religion
religion
religion
religion
religion
religion
religion
religion
religion
religion
religion
religion

YET NO MATTER HOW
DEEPLY I GO INTO MYSELF,
MY GOD IS DARK, AND LIKE
A WEBBING MADE OF A
HUNDRED ROOTS THAT
DRINK IN SILENCE.

—Rainer Maria Rilke

CONSULTING THE SILENCE— A GUIDED EXERCISE

Believe those who are seeking the truth; doubt those who find it.
—ANDRÉ GIDE

We do not expect answers to the deepest questions: Do the ends justify the means? Is man one of God's blunders, or is God one of man's blunders? What did your face look like before you were born? Nor do we trust those who claim to have answers. Yet to stave off the meaninglessness of existence, we nonetheless pursue such questions. The following process of silent and soulful contemplation can help us in this undertaking.

Fix your question in your mind, focus your thoughts, and ask it out loud. As your words die away, you may hear only silence. Ask again. If again you are confronted by silence, try once more. This time put your whole being into the question. Let it wash over you, filling your awareness with a great love for the question itself. Then ask. It is common that after this third try, the answering silence will seem deafening.

Let my silences become more eloquent.

THE ECONOMICS OF SPIRITUALITY

The meek shall inherit the Earth but not the mineral rights.
—J. PAUL GETTY

Though we are different by birth, background, and life experience, we are all creatures of the same spirit. Although some of us are young and some old, some white and some black, some rich and some poor, some very rich and some very poor, some extremely rich and some extremely poor, some disgustingly filthy rich beyond human reason and some appallingly miserably poor beyond human comprehension—we are all children of the Universe. Whether we receive our livelihood through a begging bowl, paycheck, or trust fund, we're told that there's a channel connecting each of us to the source of creation. We're told that when our channel is open, money will flow into our life; and when our channel is blocked, the money will stop flowing. We soon notice, however, that no matter how blocked some people's channels get, money still flows through their trust fund.

When my channel is blocked, will money still flow through my trust fund?

REASONING WITH YOUR
INNER PROPHET

> Jesus promised those who would follow his leadings only three things:
> that they should be absurdly happy, entirely fearless, and always in
> trouble.
> —MARTY BABCOCK

Each of us is caught in a tug of war between our inner prophet and
our virtual adult. When your inner prophet is strong, you are seized
with a burning, lucid vision of who you must become, and you follow it. But the world resists. Sooner or later, no matter how strong
you are, you will face a moment of weakness when your virtual
adult comes wafting through your brain like the smell of hospital
food. "Don't be a fool," it whispers. "Listen to reason." But you must
not listen. You mustn't let the world set the rules. Better to go forward and face the consequences, for reason always means what
someone else has to say, and a prophet must change the world in
order to be at home in it.

When I don't listen to reason, reason listens to me.

SKEPTICAL MYSTICISM

It takes faith to believe, and it takes courage not to, and who is to say
which is the deeper and more truthful.
—HERBERT WEISINGER

You often hear about believers who have a crisis of faith, but what
of the skeptics among us who have a crisis of doubt? For years we
skeptics have decisively refuted the metaphysical claims of the great
religions and scoffed at the pretensions of newfangled spiritual
fashions. But then our doubts are suddenly shaken by an unbidden
mystical experience. The power of this direct cognition of ultimate
reality, beyond word or image, is undeniable. But does it prove the
existence of God? If you remain skeptical, you find yourself in a difficult state. You now seriously doubt your doubt and yet have no
abiding faith to replace it. How do you proceed? You can no longer
be atheistic because you've communed with the divine. You can't
be religious because the existence of God is still in question; what's
more, religious representations of God now get in the way of your
direct mystical experience. Nor can you be agnostic because you're
far from neutral on the subject. You must become a skeptical mystic. As you cut your own singular path to the great whatever, you

must now treat your own experiences with the relentless skepticism you once reserved for the claims of others.

I am One with a God I do not believe in.

DIVING INTO THE ABYSS

Faith is faith in faith.
—BROTHER VOID

Mystics, madmen, poets, and philosophers speak of the Abyss. A realm of boundless terror and harrowing self-knowledge exists within you, they say, whether you can see it or not. Those who can are both cursed and blessed. Their world is cracked open. To make things whole, they are often driven to furious art-making or ascetic devotion. Maybe you vaguely sense the presence of this Abyss in you. Maybe the next time you're deep in silent contemplation, or on drugs, or just gazing up at the endless night sky, your world is cut asunder, your soul shudders in terror, and flailing at nothingness, you fall through the groundless ground of Being toward God's implacable gaze. If this happens, what are you to do? There is no escape, they say. Fear will only drive you toward madness. Instead, with focused courage, and with faith in faith alone, you must turn around your shuddering will to face the depths, and dive.

Already falling, I choose to dive.

death
death
death
death
death
death
death
death
death
death
death
death
death
death
death
death
death
death
death
death
death
death
death
death
death
death
death
death
death
death
death
death

YOUR LIFE IS DIFFERENT
ONCE YOU GREET DEATH
AND UNDERSTAND YOUR
HEART'S POSITION.

—Louise Erdrich

EMBRACING YOUR INNER CORPSE

This thing called *corpse* we dread so much is living with us here and now.
—MILAREPA

In each of us is an inner corpse struggling to be exhumed. Unlike the corpse you will one day become, this shadow corpse is alive. It is the living presence of death that you carry within you. It is more than your certain knowledge of death's ultimate triumph; it is your portal to nothingness, the other ocean of Being. If you can find the courage to unearth and embrace your inner corpse, you can lead a more vivid, expansive, and authentic life. But if you keep your inner corpse buried away, you live a great lie. You distort your search for truth into a project of false immortality. You deny the most solemn core of your being, condemning yourself to premature cheerfulness. To the outside world you might seem healthy, happy, and success-ful—but your inner corpse might just as well be dead.

My inner corpse is not dead.

LEARNING TO DIE

To practice death is to practice freedom. A man who has learned how to die has unlearned how to be a slave.
—MICHEL DE MONTAIGNE

Death is too important to be left to the end of life. Better to face death now while you can still enjoy what it has to offer. Fortunately, there are several ways to do this, and a special outfit for each encounter. In jeans, chartreuse windbreaker, and parachute, you can dangle your legs out the doorway of an old prop plane and push yourself into oblivion. In fatigues and helmet, you can endure the daily routine of terror and courage until death is an easy friend. Sitting silently in a loose-fitting black meditation robe, you can follow your inner corpse to its ultimate ego-annihilating epiphany.

Maybe you shy away from these encounters. "I can't face the truth," you say. "It's too intense. I'd like to have a destiny, but not just yet." To find your resolve, remember what's at stake. If you push death away, you'll be plagued by the nagging dread of oblivion deferred. But when you face death now, you avoid the long wait in the chamber of fear. You turn the tables. No longer the hunted, you become the hunter. In this way you get a head start on your destiny.

Once I learn to die, I can get on with my life.

AT ONE WITH YOUR INNER CORPSE—A GUIDED MEDITATION

Of all mindfulness meditations, that on death is supreme.
—THE BUDDHA

Imagine you are a flower at the moment of death: your bright colors begin to fade, your leaves become brown and brittle, your delicate petals fall to the earth. Imagine decomposing: you feel the life milk drain from your body; the fibers of your being hemorrhage into the soil; the smell of rot fills your nostrils. Go deeper into the soil: consider the countless deaths that have enriched the moist earth around you. As you disintegrate among these ghostly tendrils, remember that you are feeding the greater harmony of the planet. Now, imagine your final moment: time itself washes into eternity; the least desire and the pettiest vanity are foregone; the darkness whispers your true name. You are One with your inner corpse.

As you go about your day, try to stay with these feelings, but make sure to monitor your body temperature regularly.

I set aside a little time each day to die.

LIVING WITH DEATH

When something rotten like this happens, then you have your choice.
You start to really be alive or you start to die. That's all.
—JAMES AGEE

The death of one you love is a terrible affirmation of life. A part of you has been murdered, an intimacy stripped from your side, leaving an unthinkable emptiness. Where have they gone? There is no answer. Such tragedy can make you fearless. It can stop the world and make everything clear. But for your heart to reckon with the true finality of this death—to hold the impossible weight of your brother's boxed ashes—you must squarely face your own mortality. Somehow, the same grief that demands this of you also lends you courage for the task.

As you survive this loss and integrate it, you find that death has a nurturing power. It takes the measure of all things and throws you back upon the joy of living. It gives you the strength to weave the darkness into the fibers of your life and go on.

The loss of someone I love reminds me why I am here.

enlightenment
enlightenment
enlightenment
enlightenment
enlightenment
enlightenment
enlightenment
enlightenment
enlightenment
enlightenment
enlightenment
enlightenment
enlightenment
enlightenment
enlightenment
enlightenment
enlightenment
enlightenment
enlightenment
enlightenment
enlightenment
enlightenment
enlightenment
enlightenment
enlightenment
enlightenment
enlightenment
enlightenment
enlightenment
enlightenment
enlightenment
enlightenment

THE ATTAINMENT OF
ENLIGHTENMENT . . .
IS THE ULTIMATE AND
FINAL DISAPPOINTMENT.

—Chögyäm Trungpa

THE AGONY OF BEING CONNECTED TO EVERYTHING IN THE UNIVERSE

What is to give light must endure burning.
—VICTOR FRANKEL

Many of us have set out on the path of enlightenment. We long for a release of selfhood in some kind of mystical union with all things. But that moment of epiphany—when we finally see the whole pattern and sense our place in the cosmic web—can be a crushing experience from which we never fully recover.

Compassion hurts. When you feel connected to everything, you also feel responsible for everything. And you cannot turn away. Your destiny is bound with the destinies of others. You must either learn to carry the Universe or be crushed by it. You must grow strong enough to love the world, yet empty enough to sit down at the same table with its worst horrors.

To seek enlightenment is to seek annihilation, rebirth, and the taking up of burdens. You must come prepared to touch and be touched by each and every thing in heaven and hell.

I am One with the Universe, and it hurts.

THE ABYSS—A mystical region of human consciousness, inducing terror, awe, and various forms of self-annihilation. As yet uncharted, due to lack of empirical data. Anecdotal evidence suggests a vortex of death and infinity enclosing the timeless center of all things. Variation: the Void.

THE BOOT CAMP OF LIFE—A traditional child-rearing practice in which the child is trained to handle the dysfunction of adult institutions by being relentlessly drilled in dysfunction by his own family.

THE COLLECTIVE UNCONSCIENCE—An unspoken, consensual hallucination of social order that permits the individual to mask any responsibility he or she might feel for government wrongdoing or social ills in a web of numbed-out apathy and mass denial.

COMPASSIONATE NIHILISM—A moral philosophy that permits the individual to love the world in spite of the obvious meaninglessness of all existence. Popular among professional social-justice activists who have given up hope but can't think of anything better to do.

DAILY AFFLICTION—A tiny manifesto summarizing a painfully sublime condition of human existence so as to better prepare the individual for the jungle of existential terror and paradox that awaits with each new day.

DESTRUCTIVE VISUALIZATION—An auto-suggestive technique in which the individual forms a mental image of the worst imaginable outcome for the given situation and uses this as an impetus for taking action to prevent it from happening.

THE INNER ARTIST—The aspect of man as "creator," as distinct from the poor, hapless, unformed "creature" aspect of man that the "creator" aspect of man will brutally refashion into a unique and irreplaceable being. While your inner artist is under the influence of abstract expressionism, do not drive or operate heavy machinery.

THE INNER BIGOT—An unconscious psychological projection whereby those features of the Other denigrated in the self become the target of fear, hatred, violence, and exotic fascination. If not controlled, can lead to cross-burnings or clueless white rap artists.

THE INNER CORPSE—A figurative device representing the living presence of death in the unconscious mind.

THE INNER CRITIC—A self-correcting mechanism of personality growth, dispensing disapproval, doubt, character assassination, and a few invaluable pointers on form.

THE INNER PROPHET—An implacable psychological drive to reshape the world according to the individual's own inner necessity. Inner necessities may vary from individual to individual. Do not conflate with inner fanatic.

THE INNER PSYCHOPATH—A disruptive cathexis of antisocial desire, kept in check by consensual taboos of improper elevator etiquette, yet liable to erupt at any time.

THE INTERSTATE OF LIFE—An allegorical device representing the interminable and enigmatic pathways an individual must wander during his short time on Earth.

IRONIC FAITH—A philosophical position adopted by those who believe in something but also believe that it is naive and dangerous to believe in anything.

THE NAUSEA OF LANGUAGE—An experience, often induced by spelling errors, in which the decentered and undecidable fluidity of language is experienced to such an acute and catastrophic degree that the individual's own meaning-making capacities are temporarily suspended.

NEGATIVE THINKING—An eclectic collection of discredited left-brained problem-solving strategies, including debate, disagreement, criticism, and analysis.

THE OTHER SIDE OF LOVE—A phase in a love relationship when the immense erotic energy gathered over years of tenderness, caring, and sensitivity crosses over into a bitterness and frustration of equal ferocity.

SATURN'S RETURN—An astrological event marked by the completion of a full 29.6-year orbit (thus "Return") by the planet Saturn (thus "Saturn").

As a powerful sign of order and disorder, Saturn is thought to be the arbiter of a person's public self, but is actually a colossal hunk of frozen ammonia ringed by rings. Saturn's 29.6-year cycle neatly corresponds with a transition point in the human developmental life cycle when, according to Gertrude Stein, "all the whirlwind energies thrown off in the making of a personality must focus and take definite form."

SKEPTICAL MYSTICISM—A theological stance that permits the individual to hold two divergent epistemologies (a hard-line anti-metaphysical skeptical materialist socio-historical empiricism and an immanent ontological existentialist phenomenology of divine revelation and transcendence) without the individual's head exploding.

THE SUBURB WITHIN—A state of mind marked by flight from Otherness and an unwillingness to venture beyond a convenient proximity to certain household appliances.

THE SUPERMARKET OF LIFE—A realm of false choice, akin to the Buddhist labyrinth of maya, projected by ordinary consciousness and perpetuated by the tendency of advanced consumer capitalism to extend the commodity relationship into every sphere of daily life and thought. Can be overcome only through an incorruptible dedication to social revolution, sainthood, or the making of truly singular, thoroughly unmarketable works of art.

THE VIRTUAL ADULT—A socially punitive negative-feedback system known to reproduce the psychological conditions required for participation in schemes of behavior currently deemed sane.

guide to sources
guide to sources
guide to sources
guide to sources
guide to sources

The Book of Daily Afflictions is deeply influenced by the Western existentialist thought of Søren Kierkegaard, Friedrich Nietzsche, Franz Kafka, Albert
Camus, and Jean-Paul Sartre to the point where the afflictions could be accu-
rately described as "dark, twisted, existential manifestos." The existential psy-
chologists that followed in their path—Victor Frankel, Erich Fromm, R. D.
Laing, et al.—also exercised a strong influence. Selective strands in post-
modern thought, Marxism, Buddhism, and the crazy wisdom traditions of
both East and West have left their mark, as have a miscellaneous grab bag of
novelists, poets, pranksters, mystics, artists, revolutionaries, theologians, and
mad German philosophers. One mad German philosopher in particular.

The subtle exposition of New Age metaphysics in the book is informed
by many of the following popular self-help titles: *101 Uses For a Dead Angel,
Adult Children of Normal Parents, Cellulite Prophecy, Getting in Touch with Your
Inner Bitch, I Am My Own Best Casual Acquaintance, I Feel Much Better Now
That I've Given Up Hope, Meditations for Miserable People Who Want to Stay
That Way, Beyond Good and Evil, Thus Spake Zarathustra, The Genealogy of
Morals, Today I Will Nourish My Inner Martyr, Healing Your Inner Dog,* and
Brother Void's personal favorite, *Petted by the Light: The Most Profound and
Complete Feline Near-Death Experiences Ever.*[1]

Unlike most books of inspiration, the afflictions are also informed by
works critical of the genre, including hard-hitting exposés such as *I'm*

---

[1] These books actually exist.

Dysfunctional, You're Dysfunctional: The Recovery Movement and Other Self-Help Fashions, by Wendy Kaminer. *The Skeptical Inquirer,* a bimonthly magazine put out by the Committee for the Scientific Investigation of Claims of the Paranormal, proved to be a great source for reasoned critique and debunking of the latest trends regarding UFOs, ESP, astrology, miracles, magical thinking, pseudoscience, and the like. As for philosophically exposing the anti-scientific metaphysics that often passes for common wisdom, the steady hand of Carl Sagan was of invaluable assistance. As was the bloody pen of Friedrich Nietzsche.

As for the intractable problems of the human condition, the following works were instructive and sobering by their titles alone: *The Importance of Disappointment,* by Ian Craib; *Shaving the Inside of Your Skull,* by Mel Ash; and *The Trouble with Being Born,* by E. M. Cioran.

The chapter on love was to some degree informed by Roland Barthe's *A Lover's Discourse* and Rilke's much-admired *Letters to a Young Poet.* For more in-depth knowledge on the problems of love, one need look no further than one's own battered heart. Completely useless on the subject of love is any work by Friedrich Nietzsche.

The theme of "losing oneself in order to (maybe) find oneself" that is woven throughout The Book of Daily Afflictions finds its touchstone in José Ortega y Gasset's celebrated passage from *The Revolt of the Masses:*

> The man with the clear head is the man who ... looks life in the face, realizes that everything in it is problematic, and feels himself lost. And this is the simple truth—that to live is to feel oneself lost—he who accepts it has already begun to find himself, to be on firm ground. Instinctively, as do the shipwrecked, he will look round for something

to which to cling, and that tragic, ruthless glance, absolutely sincere, because it is a question of his salvation, will cause him to bring order into the chaos of his life. These are the only genuine ideas; the ideas of the shipwrecked. All the rest is rhetoric, posturing, farce. He who does not really feel himself lost is without remission; that is to say, he never finds himself, never comes up against his own reality.

A further influence (one that, without mixing metaphors, meshes neatly with Ortega y Gasset's "ideas of the shipwrecked") is found in the commandment to "Sail your ships into uncharted seas," a commandment formulated by Friedrich Nietzsche, who formulated many such commandments.

The rich textures of darkness that pervade The Book of Daily Afflictions are cast by the overlapping shadows of several towering spirits. The curved spectral darkness in Tao-like balance with its other nature, light, is cast by Ursula Le Guin. The wispy gray darkness of the Shadow Figure is Carl Jung. The pitch-black, 3-in-the-morning, broke-in-Hoboken darkness comes from Henry Miller. The predawn darkness of the rising Anti-Christ is, of course, Friedrich Nietzsche.

Beyond Brother Void's fifteen-plus years of experience as a social activist, important political influences include Abbie Hoffman, Rosa Luxembourg, Camus (particularly in The Rebel), Rudholf Bahro, Andre Gorz, and the poet of commodities himself, Karl Marx. A more recent hero is Sub-Commandante Marcos, whose Zapatista Revolution has reinvented hope in a way that perhaps even Camus could get behind. Whether Franz "There Is Hope, but Not for Us" Kafka could get behind it is another matter. Another important influence—once the power-crazed proto-Nazi theoretician of the Master

Race turned out to be a misunderstood anti-statist—was Friedrich Nietzsche.

The idea of compassionate nihilism owes a great debt to the thought and lyrics of Gandhi, Jesus, Camus, and Sid Vicious, particularly Gandhi, Jesus, and Camus. Sid Vicious was helpful, but mostly with the nihilism aspect.

The idea of ironic faith in general owes a sizable share of its inspiration to Kierkegaard. As a specific problem of contemporary society, several works proved immensely helpful, including *Post-Modernism and the World's Religions*, by Huston Smith; as well as Tom Beaudoin's intriguing investigation, *Virtual Faith: The Irreverent Spiritual Quest of Generation X*. Also of great assistance was Umberto Eco's amusing Postscript to *The Name of the Rose* and Richard Rorty's *Contingency, Irony, and Solidarity*, particularly the essay "Ironists and Metaphysicians." Charles McGrath's article in the *New York Times*, "No Kidding: Does Irony Illuminate or Corrupt?" (August 5, 2000), was an excellent contribution to the debate as it has recently crystallized around Jedediah Purdy and Dave Eggers. Friedrich Nietzsche, though he never wrote for the *New York Times*, nonetheless managed to show up 319 times on a recent Lexis-Nexis search.

On the problem of mysticism in general, Brother Void's own experiences have been the single strongest influence on the text. However, he relied heavily on certain works to situate these experiences within the broader scope of spiritual tradition and psychological theory (thus refuting his alternative theory that the CIA had implanted a "religious experience" chip in his brain). These works include Rudolf Otto's *The Idea of the Holy*, Paul Tillich's *The Courage to Be*, Rilke's *The Notebooks of Maltes Lourids Brigge*, and Robert Kegan's *There the Dance Is: Religious Dimensions of a Developmental Framework*. Also of some use was *Spiritual Emergency*, by

Stanislav Grof[2]; and *Dialogues with a Modern Mystic,* an interview with the Anglo-Indian mystic and scholar Andrew Harvey. Poetry played a role, as well, particularly T. S. Eliot's "Burnt Norton," which provided a kind of architecture of the Void, several passages from Friedrich Holderin, and an untitled and largely unknown sonnet by Genevieve W. Foster copied out of a rare volume found in the back of a used bookstore in Birmingham, Alabama. Rumi, however, has proved far too joyous, inspired, ecstatic, and positive for Brother Void at this point in his spiritual development.

The specific conception of skeptical mysticism was strongly influenced by Peter Berger's "inductive faith" as elaborated in *A Rumor of Angels.* (Inductive faith moves from human experience to statements about God, whereas deductive faith moves from statements about God to interpretations of human experience.) *The Varieties of Religious Experience,* William James's landmark study of religious experience from a phenomenological and empirical perspective, was consulted often. The more recent *Skeptics and True Believers,* by Chet Raymo, also proved helpful, as did the work of another philosopher—the great German prose stylist, the most dangerous man in Europe, that lonely syphilis-wracked argonaut of the spirit— Friedrich Nietzsche, who curiously referred to himself as the "Holy Skeptic."

On the problem of death, the work of Camus is revealing, as is the work of anybody from Tibet. In spite of their size, *The Big Book of Death* and *The Encyclopedia of Death*[3] left Brother Void a little cold. And being a relative

---

[2] Those experiencing a Void-like ontological shock (or loss of faith, existential crisis, psychic opening, or other altered state) can seek assistance through an information and referral service at the Spiritual Emergence Network founded by Stanislav Grof. Call (415) 648-2610 or email sen@ciis.edu.

[3] These books actually exist, as well.

expert on near-death experiences himself, he detected a false note in the huge popularity of books such as *Embraced by the Light,* by Betty J. Eadie, sensing in such blissful and literal accounts a near-death experience that never came quite near enough. He drew most heavily on two classics: Michel de Montaigne's famous *Essays* and Ernest Becker's Pulitzer Prize–winning work *The Denial of Death.* When it comes to death, Martin "Death is Being's ownmost possibility" Heidegger is also pretty good for a choice line or two.

On the problem of the agony of being connected to everything in the Universe, aside from Philip K. Dick, strong influences include several bad tabs of acid.

As for Friedrich Nietzsche himself, Penguin's *A Nietzsche Reader,* edited and translated by R. J. Hollingdale, proved to be a most useful short selection of Nietzsche's best work. Several treatments of Nietzche's thought, including Ronald Hayman's *Nietzsche* from the Great Philosophers series and *Introducing Nietzsche,* by Laurence Gane and Kitty Chan, are both brief and excellent. Walter Kaufman, though partial to the "good Nietzsche," is unmatched in the English language for his overall treatment of Nietzsche's life and work. His *Nietzsche: Philosopher, Psychologist, Anti-Christ* is particularly impressive. As is, of course, any work by Friedrich Nietzsche himself.

A NOTE REGARDING QUOTATIONS

The quotations used herein were collected over many years from many sources. Several books were quite helpful. One book helped immensely: *Sunbeams: A Book of Quotations,* edited by Sy Safransky, publisher of the bimonthly magazine *The Sun,* whose back page is also an excellent source.

Other useful sources are *The Dark Side; Thoughts on the Futility of Life from the Ancient Greeks to the Present,* compiled by Alan R. Pratt; *The Portable Curmudgeon,* by Jon Winokur; and *The Devil's Dictionary,* by Ambrose Bierce. *Crazy Wisdom,* by Wes "Scoop" Nisker, is also an excellent source. As is any work by Friedrich Nietzsche.

acknowledgments
acknowledgments
acknowledgments
acknowledgments
acknowledgments

Immeasurable thanks to all of you:

Andy Hermann, Anne MacKinnon, Chris Faber, David Behrstock, David Cash, Janice Fine, Jeff Gates, Ken Jordan, Kosta Demos, Lee Winkelman, Meridith Levy, Michael Barrish, Mickle Maher, Mike Prokosch, Morgan J. Meis, Pagan Kennedy, and Rachel Antell for your counsel, friendship, generous collaboration, and willingness to edit (and re-edit, and re-re-edit) the manuscript. I am truly grateful.

Carin Schiewe, Chuck Collins, David Rakoff, Harry Levinson, Jenny Levison, Kim Pfister, Kristin Barrali, Pat Nixon, Peter Laarman, Scoop Nisker, Steve Wilson, and Tory Griffith for all your support along the way.

Alane Mason for seeing what was right and making me struggle.
Joe Spieler for pushing for a better truth.

Bill All for grokking the laptop.
John Fulbrook III for several ineffably wrong flowers.
Laura Wulf for her camera and the eye behind it.
Leelo Märjamaa-Reintal for making it pop.
Liz Canner for conspiring in certain love afflictions.
Louise Schwartz for being more brutal than my inner critic.

Lynne Aston and Shira Karman for fortifying me against the Void.

Nathan Mehl for hosting the Church of Skeptical Mysticism.

Pam Kisch for forgiving me for not acknowledging her in the last book.

Seigrid Goldiner for "ragout."

Ada Muellner, Anna and Franceline Lappe, Fred Jordan, Gail Leondar-Wright, Matt Lazure, Micki McGee, Traci Nagle, Nancy Palmquist, and Stefanie Diaz for this and that and the other thing.

Peter Barnes and the Mesa Refuge for a place to write.

Harriet, Sheila, Ben, and the Blue Mountain Center for another place to write.

We all wrote this together. Thank you.

Thanks also to the following thinkers for the following thoughts:

Carl Jung: "One does not become enlightened by imagining figures of light, but by making the darkness conscious."

John Mason Brown: "The only true happiness comes from squandering ourselves for a purpose."

Victor Frankel: "Happiness cannot be pursued; it can only ensue."

Henry Moore: "The secret of life is to have a task, something you devote your entire life to, something you bring everything to, every minute of the day for your whole life. And the most important thing is—it must be something you cannot possibly do."

Theodore Roethke: "May my silences become more accurate."

Elizabeth Cleghorn Gaskell: "I'll not listen to reason. Reason always means what someone else has got to say."

Andrew Harvey: "A mystical experience is a direct cognition of ultimate reality, beyond word or image."

Buddhist adage: "Death is too important to be left to the end of life."

Glenda Taylor: "It's fearful to know we are connected to everything in the universe because then we're responsible."

index
index
index
index
index

A

abyss 91
  diving into 78
  gazing into xix
acid
  bad tabs of 100
affliction xiii, xix, 91, 95
  sufficiently severe xv
  the right one xv
agony xix, 37, 89, 100
anguish 13, 42
annihilation xxiv, 82, 89
anxiety
  essential condition of 14
apathy 91
apocalypse xxvii, 57

B

bad trip 65
bitch
  drunken, moody son-of-a 9
bitterness 37, 93
blunders 73
burdens 89

C

calamity 19
catastrophe 93

  total 41
chaos xiv, 70
cheerfulness
  premature 81
confusion xviii
crisis
  deeper into 13
  existential 99
  no way back from 13

D

damage 28
danger 93, 99
dark side
  suppressed power of xv
darkness xv, xvii, 84, 85, 97
  ensnared in 22
  heart of 10
  path of 50
death xix, xx, xxiii, xxv, 33, 47, 85, 91, 99
  denial of xxiii
  facing it now 82
  moment of 84
  nearness to 100
  presence of xxii, 81, 92
  ultimate triumph of 81
decomposing 84

Laura Wulf

about the author

Andrew Boyd is a writer and activist living in New York. As Phil T. Rich, he served as co-chair of "Billionaires for Bush (or Gore)." He is also the author of *Life's Little Deconstruction Book* and *The Activist Cookbook*.

To connect to the agony of being connected to everything in the universe, visit www.dailyafflictions.com.